THE BABYLONIAN PROPHECY

A Warning
America Must Head!

THE BABYLONIAN PROPHECY

A WARNING
AMERICA MUST HEAD!

By

Susan K. Reidel

LOGOS TO RHEMA PUBLISHING
Tulsa, Oklahoma

The Babylonian Prophecy

A Warning America Must Heed!

By Susan K. Reidel

Copyright ©2004
Library of Congress Control Number:
2004099528

International Standard Book Number:
0-9718542-7-0

ALL RIGHTS RESERVED

No part of this publication (book) may be reproduced, stored in a retrieval system, or be transmitted in any form, or by any means, electronic, mechanical, photocopying or otherwise without the prior written consent of the author, Susan K. Reidel or the publisher, Logos to Rhema Publishing.

Written permission must be secured from the publisher or author to use or reproduce any part of this book, except for the inclusion of brief quotations in critical reviews or articles.

Scripture quotations noted NIV are taken from the Holy Bible, New International Version® Copyright 1973, 1978, 1984, by the International Bible Society. Used by permission of Zondervan Bible Publishing House. All rights reserved.

The "NIV" and "New International Version" trademarks are registered in the United States Patent and Trademark Office by the International Bible Society.

Unless otherwise noted, all Scripture quotations are from the New King James Version of the Bible ©1979, 1980, 1982, 1984, by Thomas Nelson, Inc., Publishers.

Published by Logos to Rhema Publishing
7822 E. 100th St. Tulsa, Oklahoma 74133
Publisher website: logostorhema.com
Author email: sreidel@hotmail.com

Printed in the United States of America

Contents

	Preface	11
Chapter One	The Patch Removed: Seeing Clearly	13
Chapter Two	No! We Won't Go	19
Chapter Three	Wickedness Lives in Babylon	25
Chapter Four	The Epic of Gilgamesh	33
Chapter Five	The Firey Furnace	37
Chapter Six	A Tale of Two Cities	45
Chapter Seven	Looking Back to See the Future	53
Chapter Eight	What is About to Happen in Iraq?	61
Chapter Nine	Will America Heed Jeremiah's Warning?	69
Chapter Ten	Like Sodom and Gomorrah Destruction Comes	75
Chapter Eleven	My People in the Midst of Her	81
	About the Author	87

Acknowledgments

Thank you for all your help! I truly am grateful to friends and family for all their kind and loving support.

E-mail: sreidel@hotmail.com

Dedication

I would like to take the time to express thanks for every person in the ministry of Jesus Christ and doing what you believe God has told you to do. You are an incredible army and that victory for our Savior is guaranteed.

I would also like to thank the families that have encouraged my ministry throughout the years and especially Dave and Vera Roberts. You'll never know how much your faithfulness and sacrifice means to me. God know your hearts and I just want to remind you He is faithful and knows your every need.

Susan K. Reidel

Preface

As you begin to read this book I would just like to make a few comments. The book was written as a warning and is not meant to be an in depth Bible study. It is to be read, considered and prayed over for your own understanding.

I know that many people reading this book might not agree with it, but I stand in faith believing what has been written. More than anything, I hope and pray that the book will lead each and every reader to a deeper walk in Jesus Christ. For those who might not know this wonderful Savior I pray that you will find Him and know Him and realize he is just waiting for you to come home!

Chapter One

The Patch Removed: Seeing Clearly

There is a profound truth that has been overlooked by many prophecy teachers. It is only recently, as I have studied the prophets of the Bible, that I have come to an understanding that is shocking and a great warning for the world–and yet at the same time, a tremendous opportunity for America. It appears that many prophecy teachers have had very clear vision concerning what the scriptures say about Jerusalem and Israel, but not what the scriptures say about Babylon and Iraq. It now seems to me that we have been wearing a patch over one eye. We have not seen the "whole" prophetic picture with 20/20 vision. It is my desire, by writing the book, to remove the patch and let you see clearly what I believe the scriptures tell. Perhaps for the first time, you will realize where we are in the prophetic plan of God, for America, and the return of Jesus Christ to this world.

I believe that we need to take the patch off and observe God dealing with two specific cities and nations in the last days. We knew from scriptures that Israel would become an independent nation again and that Jerusalem would come under the control of Israel again. We knew that the Jewish remnant would come back and that the land would blossom again. It has been our generations privilege to see it for ourselves, but we have left out the other city and nation that God was very adamant about, Babylon and Iraq. We have failed to watch for the Prophetic scenario involving this city and nation. The premise of this prophetic insight is one of those, "You can't see the forest because of all the trees," kind of revelations. Nevertheless, I believe you will see it distinctly as the scriptures are illuminated to manifest understanding of how Babylon and Iraq are specific, prophetic, and major players on the face of the earth just before Christ gives Israel her complete and final victory!

It's interesting to look for a moment, at the biblical history of Iraq:

The Garden of Eden was created and placed in what is now the nation of Iraq. Adam and Eve were created in Iraq. Mesopotamia or the Fertile Crescent, a narrow strip of land, which was fruitful, pleasant and home of ten ancient and beginning civilizations, is in Iraq. History actually began in Iraq.

It's very important to realize that the study of history is really the study of "His Story!" We must put on the glasses of God's perspective to make sense out of the time that God has given to man and how God will redeem man in the end. As we look at the past we should get a transparent picture for the present. Understanding the times we live in, as well as the hope for the future.

It is scripture that is *the* absolute truth. What the Bible says is the truth. That might be hard to believe because what most people hear daily are the half truths, deceptions, and false doctrines of politicians, scientists, educators, kings, and world leaders as they interpret truth for their own benefit. As we apply the scriptures to the events that are taking place today, as well as in the past, we see how the word becomes the revealed truth to us.

It was in Iraq that we find:

Noah's story unfold. The Tower of Babel being built. Abraham called out of the Ur, which is the southern part of

Iraq. Rebekah, Isaac's wife, is from Nahor. Jacob meets his future wife Rachel in Iraq and Jonah preached probably the greatest sermon ever heard in Nineveh, a city of Iraq! Daniel spent the night with lions in a den in Iraq. Shadrach, Meshach and Abednego were in the fiery furnace of Iraq. Belshazzar, the King of Babylon, saw the awesome finger of God write upon the walls and tell of his kingdom's demise. Ezekiel preached in Iraq. the Wise Men came from Iraq. Peter preached in Iraq. The confusion of language took place in Iraq. And one of the first world Empires was in Iraq!

The events of Esther take place in Iraq. Nahum, one of the Minor Prophets, writes about the judgment coming in Iraq. Assyria, in Iraq, conquered the ten tribes of Israel. Amos, the herdsman prophet, cried out to God from Iraq. And probably the biggest event to take place in Iraq—it's the first place Satan shows up on the face of the earth! Satan shows up to deceive Adam and Eve, destroy God's creation and try to destroy God's prophetic plan!

The Bible is probably the greatest historic document that man has today. It tells very clearly about the origin of the universe and the creation of man. It is interesting to realize the character traits of man because the scriptures tell us he was created in the image of God. Man has language and the ability to think. He has the ability to distinguish right from wrong and more importantly, God left man with the ability of free choice!

Here in the realm of free choice is where man failed miserably. When Adam and Eve sinned it had terrible consequences, they were removed from the garden. God did not abandon man because of his sin, but gave man a tremendous hope to restore him to a right relationship with God in the future. God laid out a plan in which to redeem man from their sins and restore us into forgiveness and life with Him forever.

To understand why Babylon and Iraq are so important to history, to the present and the near future we must look back and see what happened in Iraq. Understand that Iraq was the place the first act of rebellion against God took place! God had commanded that Adam and Eve could not eat of the forbidden fruit. They did. This was a direct act of disobedience to God.

Many people wonder why there are wars, famines, diseases, revolutions, and even terrible deaths. The simple answer is , man's first sin was *rebellion* and that *sin of rebellion* was passed down through the pages of history. Man, with free choice and rebellion against God's ways, has always brought pain and suffering to the world. But remember, God made man in His image and so we also have the pages of history turning, with tremendous good that man has accomplished in obedience to the Word of God.

Man has accomplished great and wonderful things; inventions, art, music, and literature to name a few. We have touched the wonders and mysteries of heaven with outer–space programs. Men have done heroic and courageous deeds for thousands of years. Yet, I would say the best and most powerful example of God's plan of redemption for man, is that He gave us the ability to love and to receive love. Love is probably the most potent force on the face of the earth to do good!

It is astonishing how much history has taken place in Iraq. Even now the United States have troops in Iraq. America is at war. American men and women are thousands of miles away in Iraq because God stirred leaders in our country to commit there. Their might be all kinds of reasons politically, emotionally, nationally or personally for being in Iraq, but ultimately it is part of the prophetic plan of God for America. We must pray and discern what that plan is and obey it!

The nation most mentioned in scripture is Israel. But the nation that comes in second is Iraq! The scriptures use names such as, Babylon, Land of Shinar and Mesopotamia. In fact, Babylon is mentioned over 280 times in the bible. What I find more amazing is that most of those scriptures deal with a Iraq and Babylon that is only

The Patch Removed: Seeing Clearly

now coming into its prophetic importance. It boils down to this, Jerusalem and Israel have very specific promises of victory when Jesus returns to judge the world. But scriptures clearly state that Babylon and Iraq will be utterly and completely destroyed in the last days!

We need to look at the prophecies concerning Iraq and Israel and find out what is required of us as God's people. It is when we begin to grasp the reality of the scriptures concerning Iraq and Israel that we will see how truly close we are to the coming of the Lord!

This book is written to open up the understanding of the reader and clearly call the reader to remove the patch of the one-eyed approach to prophecy. Watching Jerusalem and Israel exclusively, will cause us to fail to see distinctly, with 20/20 vision, the explicit scriptures that pertain to Iraq and Bible prophecy.

It will shock you as you read about the coming destruction of Iraq. Where it will come from and the warning to everyone to *get out, flee, or be destroyed along with her*. Right at the moment, we are in a divine assignment of God for the people of Iraq. Only time will tell if man's free choice will again cause rebellion to rule the day—and the correction for such arrogance, one of complete devastation.

Hang on, you're in for a wild ride through the portals of "His Story" and how Babylon and Iraq are part of this great and divine plan of God's to save and revenge Israel!

†

*"So Jeremiah wrote in a book **all the evil that would come upon Babylon**, All these words that are written again Babylon.*

*And Jeremiah said to Seraiah, 'When you **arrive** in Babylon (America is there now) and **see** it, and **read** all these words;*

Then you shall say, 'O Lord, You have spoken against this place to cut it off, so that none shall remain in it, neither man nor beast, but it shall be desolate forever.'

*Now it shall be , **when you have finished reading this book,** that you shall tie a stone to it and throw it out into the Euphrates.*

*Then you shall say, **"Thus Babylon shall sink and not rise from the catastrophe that I will bring upon her. And they shall be weary."' Thus far are the words of Jeremiah.***

Jeremiah 51:60-64 NKJV

Chapter Two

No! We Won't Go

"Then the Lord saw that the wickedness of man was great in the earth, and that every intent of the thought of his heart was only evil continually. And the Lord was sorry that He had made man on the earth, and He was grieved in His heart. So the Lord said, 'I will destroy man whom I have created from the face of the earth, both man and beast, creeping thing and birds of the air, for I am sorry that I have made them.' But Noah found grace in the eyes of the Lord." Genesis 6:5-8 NKJV

Here is one of the most incredible stories of the Bible. God looked at what He had created, and then—because of the wickedness of men, He decided to destroy everything! God does and will judge man again for the rebellion and wickedness in the world today. But like Noah's rescue He has a plan for every person who will confess their sin, turn from their wicked ways and receive the free grace Jesus offers them as the way of escape.

Noah went into the ark with family and animals and waited for God to open the ark and start the prophetic plan for "His Son," through the seed of the future Abraham, to come and redeem man to God.

Genesis 8:15-17, 20 tells us:

> *"Then God spoke to Noah, saying, 'Go out of the ark, you and your wife, and your sons and your sons' wives with you. Bring out with you every living thing of all flesh that is with you: birds and cattle and every creeping thing that creeps on the earth, so that they may abound on the earth, and be fruitful and multiply on the earth.' ...**Then Noah built an altar to the Lord...**"* NKJV

God made it very clear to Noah that he was to scatter over all the earth and replenish it. This was part of God's great prophetic plan. God commanded man to scatter—and He expected man to obey.

In a grateful heart Noah built an alter to the Lord. Unfortunately, it didn't take long before sin was again showing its ugly side. Noah gets drunk and Ham, one of Noah's three sons, saw him naked and didn't cover him. Instead he goes to Japheth and Shem, Noah's other sons and tells them all about it.

After the flood Noah and his family begin the work of repopulating the earth. All the descendants of the earth come from Noah and his three sons. Cush, one of Ham's sons, had a son named Nimrod.

As Noah and his family moved from the ark they came to the area we call Mesopotamia, or the Plain of Shinar, in Iraq. It is here that Nimrod decides to build a tower to heaven. This is the introduction to the philosophy of Humanism.

It is interesting that Noah had built an altar to the Lord to worship God for His grace to Noah's family. *But man's rebellion will never recognize worship of God, only the worship of their own hands!*

Humanism puts man on the throne because of his accomplishments and abilities, all God given, but not God recognized.

Genesis 11:1-4 gives us the account of the Tower of Babel:

> *"Now the whole earth had one language and one speech. And it came to pass, as they journeyed from the east, that they*

found a plain in the land of Shinar, and they dwelt there. Then they said to one another, 'Come, let us make bricks and bake then thoroughly.' They had brick for stone, and they had asphalt for mortar. And they said, 'Come, let us build ourselves a city, and a tower whose top is in the heavens; **lest we be scattered abroad over the face of the whole earth."** NKJV

This act of building the tower into heaven to create a name—and a city, was total and complete rebellion against God, who had commanded them to go and fill the earth. *There would be a city,* whose maker was God, that would be established, and a nation that God would call His very own. **That city was Jerusalem and that nation was Israel.** Iraq and Babylon were the nation and city that stood against the living God. God came down and said, "No" to their plans and "No" to their rebellion. God said, "Scatter!"

There are several important things we need to look at now, to understand the Babylonian Prophecy later. First, Nimrod's name means "the rebel." He forsook the altar that Noah had built to worship and give thanks to God and decided to make a tower reaching into heaven. He knew that the tower would openly be seen as a symbol against the worship of God. It would create a name for him and establish the theme or worship based on mans efforts. Today, we call this Humanism.

This philosophy got its start with the Tower of Babel and spread throughout the world. Humanism is the attempt by man to worship or exalt himself above the knowledge of God. Nimrod became the leader of these people and the Tower of babel became the city of Babylon.

Man being praised and worshiped, became the way of thinking that has passed down to our current generation. Humanism is extremely destructive to man and to nations. It is a philosophy that God hates, and will one day be judged by the blood of His Son, Jesus Christ.

As the tower was being built God came down to see this act of disobedience.

Genesis 11:6-9 says:

> *"And the Lord said, 'Indeed the people are one and they all have one language, and this is what they begin to do; now nothing they propose to do will be withheld from them. Come, let Us go down and there confuse their language, that they may not understand one another's speech.'* ***So the Lord scattered them abroad from there over the face of all the earth.*** *And they ceased building the city. Therefore its name is called Babel because there the Lord confused the language of all the earth; and* ***from there the Lord scattered them abroad over the face of all the earth.****"* NKJV

The result of this act of rebellion against God's command to go replenish the earth, was that God confounded the people with different languages and FORCED THEM TO FULFILL HIS WORD AND SCATTER! One thing you can be sure of is—if God said it, IT'S GOING TO BE!

This is an important principle to understand if we are going to understand the Babylonian Prophecy. If God said it, that's the way it is going to be! It will not matter if we agree, see the logic, don't understand or are totally opposed to it. God has a plan and His plan will happen, just like He said it would. We cannot change His Word that has been spoken.

Some of the sons of Ham stayed in the land of Shinar (Iraq) and became known as the Sumerians. It is necessary to know this—in order to understand that Ham's generations actually became the nations that were Israel's major enemies; Egyptians, Babylonians, Assyrians, Philistines and various Cannanites.

You might ask way building the Tower of Babel was such a great sin. Yes, it was an act of rebellion, but the greater sin was the plan of satan, through Nimrod, to *stop, change and alter* the prophetic plan to bring redemption into the world through Abraham and his seed, Jesus.

Genesis 3:14-15 says:

> *"So the Lord God said to the serpent:*
> *'Because you have done this. You are cursed more than all cattle. And more than every beast of the field; On your belly you shall go, and you shall eat dust all the days of your life. And I will put enmity between you and the woman. And between your seed and her Seed; He shall bruise your head. And you shall bruise His heel.'"*
> NKJV

Remember, satan shows up first in Iraq, in the Garden of Eden. It is here that God curses satan and sets in motion the great plan for the coming of the Messiah to save mankind. Then His going back into heaven to allow the nations time to repent and receive Him. And lastly to return in triumphant glory to save and restore Israel.

The last half of the prophecy which many have failed to see—is that God also set in motion the prophetic plan for Babylon and Iraq. Which is to destroy it completely for its treatment of Israel under Nebuchadnezzar's reign.

The scriptures are clear Babylon is to be totally, completely destroyed and never to be inhabited again!

Isaiah 13:19 states the future of Babylon clearly:

> *"And Babylon, the glory of kingdoms, the beauty of the Chaldeans' pride will be as when God overthrew Sodom and Gomorrah."* NKJV

We know this is a future event because Babylon has never been overthrown like Sodom and Gomorrah! It is yet to be.

The Tower of Babel was building the stairway into heaven by the efforts and plans of man. There is only one way man will reach heaven and that is through the prophetic plan of Jesus Christ and the grace He offers to anyone who will receive Him and accept His sacrifice on the cross as the complete and total payment for their sins. You must believe that complete and total forgiveness is available to you, in order to come into the redemptive plan of God for man.

The temple of Marduk was built in the city of Babylon. This temple and its name means, "The Creator and King of the Universe." Man's belief in false gods, false religion and deception created the atmosphere for God's judgment against Babylon. Babylon in Iraq was rebellious, unholy, and brought a anti-god, Antichrist spirit into the world.

Even the hanging gardens were a man-made attempt to recreate the Garden of Eden. And even though the Hanging Gardens of Babylon were one of the Seven Wonders of the World, they were never a match to what God created in the garden of Eden, and can never match the greatest wonder, Jesus!

The remnant of people that stayed in the area of Iraq were people who had believed the lie of the Tower to make them a name, a city and receive the glory for it. They were rebellious to God's commands. They forsook the altar of God, for what they could accomplish with their own hands. Their actions were an attempt, by satan's influence, to stop the prophetic plan for Jesus, Jerusalem and Israel.

> *"The pride of your heart has deceived you, you who dwell in the clifts of the rock, whose habitation is high; you who say in your heart, 'Who will bring me down to the ground?' Though you ascend as high as the eagle and though you set your nest among the stars, from there I will bring you down, says the Lord."* Obadiah 1:3,4 NKJV

CHAPTER THREE

WICKEDNESS LIVES IN BABYLON

Prophecy is really history of the future. According to scriptures it seems the future is here and now! History is primarily a study in how God deals with nations, cultures and people. Prophecy gives us a hint of the future history of the world. Somehow, America is in a prophetic time and who would ever believe *it* would be the nation to rebuild Iraq!

These prophecies are strong warnings that America needs to heed, because God is not going to change His Word and what He has spoken over Iraq. We need to be aware of the scriptures, and prayerfully consider the grace time-frame we are in.

> *"And Babylon, the glory of kingdoms, the beauty of the Chaldeans' pride, will be as when God overthrew Sodom and Gomorrah.*
>
> *It will never be inhabited, nor will it be settled from generation to generation; nor will the Arabian pitch tents there, nor will the shepherds make their sheepfolds there.*
>
> *...Her time is near to come, and her days will not be prolonged."* Isaiah 13: 19-20, 22b NKJV

Although Babylon has been defeated in wars it was never destroyed like Sodom and Gomorra with no one inhabiting it. This is a future prophecy, and I believe America is right in the middle of that prophecy, under God's grace. But we will have to obey scriptures that tell us clearly to get out and the only way we will be able to do that safely is to turn to God with our whole hearts and pray for divine wisdom.

The Fertile Crescent is often called the Cradle of Civilization and the beginning cultures that made up this small strip of land were: *Sumerian, Akkadian, Babylonian, Hittite, Phoenician, Hebrew, Assyrian, Chaldean, Median, and Persian.*

Today, these cultures have once again been brought to the forefront of current military events. But in the past they were known for their brilliant techniques for agricultural purposes. They were known for their building of dams for flood control because the Tigris and the Euphrates annually flood in April, May and June. They built canals for irrigation and were the inventors of the wheel! They were incredible with the domestication of animals and to their credit they did follow God's command to fill the earth, subdue it and use it to benefit mankind.

Unfortunately, man was not able to subdue his rebellious nature. And because of not surrendering to the altar of the Lord—wars, revolutions, famines, and diseases came—and cultures were forced to move and start all over. Rebellion is the issue that man still deals with in his quest to forget God and refuse to acknowledge Him as Lord and King.

The Sumerians were the architects of the arch dome and built massive structures. They created temple towers called ziggurats, which were a kind of stepped up building with the top being dedicated to a false god. Many believe that the Tower of Babel was a ziggurat. These cultures were strong in education, math and science. Trade and commerce grew greatly.

Prophecy shows us that Babylon will be rebuilt and these ideas will be seen again. But one of the most interesting pieces of information I have come across is that the original Sumerian government was a form of democracy. Exactly what America is trying to establish in Iraq right now!

Samuel Noah Kramer writes: *"In the early days political power lay in the hands of these free citizens and a city governor known as ensi, who was no more than a peer among peers. In case of decisions vital to the city as a whole, these free citizens met in a bicameral assembly consisting of an upper house of 'elders' and a lower house of 'men.'"*

<small>Samuel Noah Kramer, *The Sumerians* (Chicago: The University of Chicago Press, 1963), page 74.</small>

A simple form of democracy was the beginning for Iraq. Could it be that the ending form of democracy is the last government of Iraq before this dreaded judgment happen to Babylon and Iraq?

One of the greatest achievements was under King Hammurabi. He collected the law codes of the Sumerian, Akkadian and the Babylonians. He managed to bring together over 300 laws, which be believed were necessary to bring justice in the land and to prevent the strong from oppressing the weak and to further the welfare of the people. Almost sounds like the foundation documents of America!

Look at what is stated in Zechariah 5:5-11:

> *"Then the angel who talked with me came out and said to me, 'Lift your eyes now. And see what this is that goes forth.' So I asked, 'What is it?' And he said, 'It is a basket (in Hebrew a ephah) that is going forth.' He also said, 'this is their resemblance throughout the earth: here is a lead disc lifted up, and this is a woman sitting inside the basket'; then he said, 'This is Wickedness!' And he thrust her down into the basket, and threw the lead cover over its mouth. Then I raised my eyes and looked, and there were two women, coming with the wind in their wings; for they had wings like the wings of a stork, and they lifted up the basket between earth and heaven. So I said to the angel who talked with me, 'Where are they carrying the basket?' And he said to me, 'to build a house for it in the land*

of Shinar; when it is ready, the basket will be set there on its base.'" NKJV

Zechariah was puzzled by what he saw, so he asked the angel for some guidance and understanding. The angel tells him—this woman represents wickedness. The two women are angels that come and take the ephah (economic system) and the lead lid to hold in the wickedness to Babylon where a base or foundation will be laid for it to sit upon. They are divine servants of the Lord with a duty to perform.

The main idea seems to be that wickedness is going to be taken to a place where a house has been built for it. This economic system, democratic form of government will have a foundation on which it will be built and allowed to flourish. As scripture tells us an ephah was a measure used in commerce. I believe what is going to happen in Iraq and Babylon is that she is being rebuilt into a strong economic (possibly because of her vast supply of oil), religious, and political nation. She will eventually be a very powerful and major player in Middle East politics. We have not yet seen the rebuilt Iraq, but I believe we are in the beginning stages of this new nation.

The old Iraq, was a highly formed civilization because it did have written laws and a democratic structure to enforce them. These laws made it possible for people to live together in peace and harmony. Many of Hammurabi's law codes were really found in the Biblical principle of sowing and reaping. Basically, every man would be held accountable for his or her own actions and the Ten Commandments were still the structure of law found in almost every nation of the world today. The problem Iraq had with the law was that justice was not always carried out according to the laws purpose. You can have law, but apart from the obedience to the Word of God you can never really have justice.

I find it profound that America is now in Iraq. We are helping to develop a democratic country that will again prosper, and as scripture tells us, project the wickedness of false religion, the economy of the Antichrist and the power as a nation to again become a center of

Wickedness Lives in Babylon

rebellion. God, like the Tower of Babel, will come down to see and this time take it off the face of the map, forever!

Scripture tells us that when the Antichrist is ruling he will incorporate an economic system that everyone will have to submit to if they wish they wish to buy or sell anything. Scripture is clear, a mark will be given and that is the only way you will be able to pay for your lifestyle. Without the mark of the beast you will NOT BE ABLE TO BUY OR SELL! It is fascinating that America is now fighting in Iraq. Our goal was to liberate Iraq from Saddam Husseim. Now we have expanded our original goal and are helping to establish a democratic form of government. Surprising to me is the fact that God is using America as the nation rebuilding the nation of Iraq and a place for the future Antichrist system to operate fully! One thing America needs to understand is that the Word of God is true and we cannot change the fact that wickedness will reside in Babylon!

Will wickedness' ephah's (economic system) that wickedness' foundation (democratic government) is laid upon, be this new Babylon? We must keep aware of the prophetic purpose we have for being in Iraq (which I will explain in a later chapter). What is in store for the world from this new Iraq?

For now, we must look with both eyes wide open. We must fulfill the plans we have for the war and at the same time be aware there is a prophetic plan to fulfill also.

There are specifically three main prophecies we need to comprehend to discern that the return of the Lord is imminent:

❏ Israel would have to become a nation again. That happened in 1948. No one ever thought Israel would be established again, but look at her after a short fifty-five years. She is strong militarily, the whole world looks to her for her intelligence capabilities and she is prosperous and has a permanent place in the events that transpire in the world. She may have more enemies than any other nation, but she is strong, prosperous, growing and an independent nation!

- Jerusalem would have to be in the hands of the Jewish people, and that happened in 1967!

- This message of the saving grace of Jesus Christ, the world's only hope, would be preached to all nations. With television, satellite, radio and the Internet that is almost a finished work.

*"And this gospel of the kingdom will be preached in all the world as a witness to all the nations, **and then the end will come.**"*
Matthew 24:14 NKJV

Now we come to the image that Daniel saw and realize the head, that most prophecy scholars agree was Babylon, is once again standing and will take its place in this prophetic line up as the head. It's clear that Babylon would also have to be restored in the last days just as the Medes and Persians, Greece, and the revived Roman empires would. We are now seeing the head come back into a position of leadership through establishing a democracy in Iraq that will make it a stable and strong nation. The amount of years it takes to become like Israel did in 55 years is up to God. I don't believe it is going to take that long and we should be looking up and know the time of the coming of the Lord is soon!

The Sumerian people believed that they were servants of the deity that founded the city-state they lived in. They began to worship a multitude of gods and reject the living God completely. It's at this time that God sets in motion the prophetic plan for Israel and calls Abraham, a Semite, living in Ur to leave his land. Abraham decides to obey God and leave the Sumerians of Iraq and trust God to show him a "Promised Land."

We now have Babylon and Iraq given over to idolatry, when God calls Abraham out and away from the sins of this nation. God sets in motion a prophetic plan for the redemption of the world through the SEED of Abraham and God set in motion the prophetic judgment of prophecy against Iraq and the wickedness that spread throughout the world from her.

We now live in the divine necessity of these prophecies. We can accept the grace and put God as the head or choose the Humanism of this world and put self as the head. Either way you cannot escape the prophetic plan set out for each one in the last days.

Here is a statement that is not politically correct, but nevertheless it is the truth: *God chose Abraham and prepared a place for His people, Israel; and prepared a plan for the salvation of man, including the people of Iraq.* God's heart is that everyone accept Jesus. God is not willing that any man, woman, race, or tribe be lost to the judgments coming into the world, and even now are! He has made a way of escape, even for Iraq.

God *is* the Alpha and the Omega, the Beginning and the End. Right from the beginning, God had Babylon and Iraq as well as Jerusalem and Israel as the center of Bible prophecy. This has been a struggle for thousands of years, but still the signs for being able to know when the coming of the Lord would be can be discerned a little easier as we look at these two nations side by side.

Finally, Iraq under the help of the United States is again being restored to fulfill the prophetic plan and experience the final judgment of scripture spoken against her. Israel, on the other hand, exist as a nation again waiting to see their Messiah. We must be close!

"For the Lord will have mercy on Jacob, and will still choose Israel, and settle them in their own land. The strangers will be joined with them, and they will cling to the house of Jacob. Then people will take them and bring them to their place, and the house of Israel will possess them for servants and maids in the land of the Lord; they will take them captive whose cap-

tives they were, and rule over their oppressors. It shall come to pass in the day the Lord gives you rest from your sorrow, and form your fear and the hard bondage in which you were made to serve, that you will take up this proverb against the king of Babylon, and say:

> 'How the oppressor has ceased, The golden city ceased!
> The Lord has broken the staff of the wicked, the scepter of the rulers;
> He who struck the people in wrath with a continual stroke, he who ruled the nations in anger, is persecuted and no one hinders.
> The whole earth is at rest and quiet; they break forth into singing.'" Isaiah 14:1-7 NKJV

Chapter Four

The Epic of Gilgamesh

One of the greatest inventions that came from the Sumerian dynasty was writing. Many of the old writings have been preserved and we know that Babylon was really one the most magnificent cities built. To understand present Babylon you only have to realize how important this city is. In fact, it is only about 54 miles south of modern Baghdad, between the Tigris and Euphrates rivers.

Babylon, apart from the living God and worshipping false idols created a story, a kind of Babylonian Genesis. It seems everyone wants an answer to the question, "is there life after death?" and the Sumerians were no different. This epic of Gilgamesh was written at the same time of Abraham. This poem is probably the oldest form of literature apart from the bible. So, again we see a false doctrine come out of Babylon that denied the existence of the one true living God.

The hero of the work, Gilgamesh, sets out to search for everlasting life for himself and his deceased friend, Enkidu. Gilgamesh was the king of Uruk and he is desperate in his search. He never finds the answer and so he takes on the hopelessness of life after death and turns to denial of a living God. I believe this is one of the main reasons idolatry took over Babylon!

At the same time this epic is written and being discussed culturally Abraham, a Semite living in Ur around 2,000 B.C. Hears God call him and decides to obey the one true God and leave everything he knows to trust the promises of his God.

Genesis 12:1-4a, 8 shows the experience Abraham had.

"*Now the Lord had said to Abram:*

> '*Get out of your country,*
> *From your family*
> *And from your father's house.*
> *To a land that I will show you.*
> *I will make you a great nation.*
> *I will bless you*
> *And make your name great;*
> *And you shall be a blessing.*
> *I will bless those who bless you.*
> *And I will curse him who curses you.*
> *And in you all the families of the earth will be blessed.*'

So Abram departed as the Lord had spoken to him...
And he moved from there to the mountain east of Bethel, and he pitched his tent with Bethel on the west and Ai on the east; there he built an altar to the Lord and called on the mane of the Lord." NKJV

God was speaking, Abraham was listening—and chose to obey Him. God says He will answer anyone who calls on His name.

Gilgamesh was seeking for God in all the wrong places, coming up with all the wrong conclusions, and leading a nation into deception with him. He gets so discouraged he refuses to even acknowledge that God is a possibility. He makes his own god, *I me, mine,* It sounds a little like the Epic of Gilgamesh could also be called Evolution and Humanism. These two epics have spread around the world today causing many to miss God and all the blessings He has for them.

Evolution and Humanism has the wrong premise. That wrong premise reaches the wrong conclusions, which leads people into the wrong belief system! Like Gilgamesh they will let you take a long journey of searching and seeking, but will never, *ever* lead you to the simple truth that God loves you, and all you have to do is seek His face.

Abraham obeyed and immediately set up a place to worship and honor this living God who had promised so much to him. God had a prophetic plan. You can believe the New Age authors, writing the new epics of Gilgamesh—turning thousands to false religion like the Babylonians did. Or your can look to God, who promised the eternal life that Gilgamesh was looking for, yet couldn't find.

Today, we see through prophetic eyes the fulfillment of scripture that leads us to the knowledge that Jesus Christ is the only way, the only truth and the only life!

> *"For God so loved the world that He gave His only begotten Son, that whoever believes in Him should not perish but have everlasting life.*
>
> *He who believes in Him is not condemned; but he who does not believe is condemned already, because he has not believed in the name of the only begotten Son of God."* John 3:16,18 NKJV

CHAPTER FIVE

THE FIREY FURNACE

A very interesting event happened in Daniel chapter three. It tells about how Nebuchadnezzar had built a tall statue of himself and how he demanded that everyone bow down and worship it. He had a little problem, in fact three; Shadrach, Meshach and Abednego! They refused to bow down to the image.

In Daniel 3:12 it states:

> *"There are certain Jews whom you have set over the affairs of the province of Babylon: Shadrach, Meshach, and Abed-Nego; these men, O king, have not paid due regard to you. They do not serve your gods or worship the gold image which you have set up."* NKJV

What I want you to see is that for a short season of time Nebuchadnezzar had set up government official to rule the nation from various parts who were submitted to the living God. These leaders were put in the position to save the remnant of Hebrews who had been taken captive by Nebuchadnezzar. There were still problems, but God had put people in control to turn some of the vile situations of Babylon around. Perhaps, that is the very reason America is in Iraq right now. One thing for sure is that American heroes removed the vile, tortuous, and despicable Saddam Hussein. Like the three Hebrew children; Shadrach, Meshach, and Abednego—American soldiers, with specific names, were chosen of God bring Saddam down. God is using America in strange and unusual ways.

The fiery furnace that these three men were thrown into was just the place that God used. It became the place that God used to turn a leader, Nebuchadnezzar, that was once deplorable, into a leader who recognized God. Through Gods dealing with Nebuchadnezzar, the people of Babylon were allowed to find this same God.

In Daniel 3:28-30 Nebuchadnezzar says:

> *"Nebuchadnezzar spoke, saying, 'Blessed be the God of Shadrach, Meshach, and Abed-Nego, who sent His Angel and delivered his servants who trusted in Him, and they have frustrated the king's word, and yielded their bodies, that they should not serve nor worship any god except their own God! Therefore I make a decree that any people, nation, or language which speaks anything amiss against the God of Shadrach, Meshach, and Abed-Nego shall be cut in pieces, and their houses, shall be made an ash heap; because there is no other God who can deliver like this.' Then the king promoted Shadrach, Meshach, and Abed-Nego in the province of Babylon."*
> NKJV

Take some time to review the truth Nebuchadnezzar learned from this fiery trial of the Hebrew children and the miraculous salvation of their God for them.

(1)   He blessed. God
(2)   He realized God had angels and sent them to help his children.
(3)   He understood that God delivers His Servants.
(4)   He understood that God rewards trust in Him.

(5) *He recognized that this miracle changed his (Nebuchadnezzar's) way of thinking and he was willing to change his commands to bless these men who stood for their God.*

(6) *He realized that these men were willing to give their life to serve their God.*

On September 11, 2001 terrorists hit the World Trade Center in New York. It was a shocking day and one we can never forget. It was a day we will grieve about for a long time to come, America never realized that anything of this sort could happen on our own soil, but it did and what good could ever come out of something so evil? Does God have a plan and did he set America on a course to be a nation He would use to fulfill Bible prophecy?

After Shadrach, Meshach, and Abednego were saved and delivered out of the fiery furnace we have seen how God was glorified. As we go on to study Daniel chapter four we find Nebuchadnezzar boasting about his prosperity and God gives him a dream. Daniel interprets the dream for him and basically says you are going to live like an animal for seven (7) years. God tells him his kingdom will be restored to him again after that period of time and that is exactly what happens.

What I want to look at here is the verse that tells why God this thing. In Daniel 4:17 it says:

"This decision is by the decree of the watchers, and the sentence by the word of the holy ones, in order that the living may know that the Most High rules in the kingdom of men, **Gives it to whomever He will** *and sets over it the lowest of men."* NKJV

It is God who is sovereign over every nation. In fact, as Nebuchadnezzar becomes an animal for seven years we know from chapter three of Daniel that God's men are helping rule a nation that had been called wicked before God. There was a space of time for *"grace,"* if you will, between Nebuchadnezzr's illness, restoration and his wicked son Belshazzar, who saw the handwriting on the wall! This grace, of a least seven years, where the Hebrew leaders were in positions of power helped to preserve the Jewish nation and put into action God's plan to keep them from perishing.

After Belshazzar parties the night away and uses the sacred temple artifacts in his wicked revelry God allows the Medes and Persians to invade Babylon and it is all over for Babylon for hundreds of years.

Lets look closely at what was taking place in Babylon at this time. Nebuchadnezzar was crazy and not running the kingdom. God's people who were in captivity, in Babylon, had come to a place of promotion, authority and were ruling. That is a picture of God's grace!

Now we see that something good did come out of the fiery furnace of pure evil. Just as we see Shadrach, Neshach and Abednego promoted to positions of authority in Iraq, so it seems America came out of her fiery furnace to be given similar positions of authority and power in Iraq. America, with her sons and daughters, took out Sad dam Hussein and now America is establishing a democratic form of government in Iraq. We are now in authority over our enemy!

The kings of terrorism said, "We will destroy America. We will cripple her. We will devastate America and her economy!" but the truth is just like the scriptures say that the king's words are changed when God is in control and like Shadrach, Meshach, and Abed-Nego the table were turned and what was meant to be destroyed by the enemy is now is authority over them!

What would be the reasoning behind this twist of fate. Well, just like the Hebrew children put in authority and rulership over the Babylonian kingdom, God is allowing Christian America to preserve and protect the people of Iraq with the gospel. We will only be allowed to stay in Iraq for a short season of time before the judgment of destruction described fully in Isaiah chapters 13 and 14 and Jeremiah chapters 50 and 51 comes.

We should see revival in Iraq as long as God leaves the door open and we are in control. I met a pastor in 2004 who told me he had seven underground churches in Iraq. At the time It thought that was good, but now, having come to the revelation of what is about to happen in Iraq, I see a great plan of god, with chosen shepherds, already preparing for the harvest in Iraq. God is not willing any should perish and He will give the nation of Iraq a time to repent and come to know the true and living God.

God was preparing even before the turn of events in the September 11 tragedy. Our enemy was saying they would destroy us and God said, *you might try, but I am sovereign over the nations and I give them to whom I will.*" America, God gave us Iraq, now let's give them the gospel, the hope and only future they have is through Jesus Christ.

When Cyrus overran Babylon and took over as the nation now looking for a world empire Daniel came into even more prominence and authority. In fact, Cyrus promoted him and Daniel told him of the prophet Isaiah and the rebuilding needed for the temple in Israel. In 536 B.C. Cyrus issued a tremendous and surprising decree!

"Thus says Cyrus king of Persia: All the kingdoms of the earth the Lord God of heaven has given me. And He has commanded me to build Him a house at Jerusalem which is in Judah. Who is among you of all His people? May the Lord his God be with him, and let him go up!" 2 Chronicles 36:23 NKJV

Daniel and the Hebrew children had kept the Word of God alive in their generation. They had been given positions of authority in enemy captivity and they were given power to fulfill their desire to rebuild the temple.

America, God has done the same thing for us, His servants. We can now go into Iraq and preach the gospel while there is time. We've been given a great opportunity and we should not miss it. It won't be easy. It wasn't easy on the Hebrew children, but God showed his faithfulness in incredible circumstances and a generation was preserved to go back and rebuild the temple!

A tremendous number of men and women volunteered for this task. Some estimates say almost 43,000 Hebrews left Babylon and went home with money that Cyrus raised for the project! The Persian Empire prospered for over two centuries. This Persian prosperity was so because scripture says that who ever blesses Israel will be blessed and who ever curses Israel will be cursed. Cyrus was a tolerant, beneficent and kind leader to the Hebrews. God blessed his kingdom because of his treatment of the Hebrews living in Babylon at that time.

What Osama bin Laden meant for evil, what Saddam Hussein meant for evil, God has changed for a good work. These terrorist leaders have had to eat their words of destruction and have them turned on them. The very thing they were trying to do to us have been done to them.

America, we need to look at what we have accomplished in the years since the attack on the World Trade Center.

- ❑ We have Liberated Afghanistan.
- ❑ We have liberated Iraq.
- ❑ We have crushed the Taliban (the ruling cruel and fundamentalist government of Afghanistan).
- ❑ We have crippled al-Qaida. Over 755 of their leadership has been captured and telling all they know!
- ❑ We have put nuclear inspectors in Libya, and that nation has disarmed from hear of what they see happening in Iraq.
- ❑ We captured a murdering, terrorist responsible for killing hundreds of thousands of people, Saddam Hussein. Who has since been

The Firey Furnace

❑ tried and executed by the new free government of Iraq.

❑ We have given the nation of Iraq a great opportunity to become a democratic nation with freedom ringing throughout the Middle East as an example of what democracy can do for a nation.

Yes, 9-11 was a horrible and tragic day for America. One day in which we will grieve a long time for the loss of life that happened in the Twin Towers, the Pentagon, and aboard the planes that went down. The enemy thought they had us, but as you can see God took us out of the fiery furnace of affliction and promoted us to take away the enemies authority and replace it with a power few will ever give up once they experience it. That power is freedom!

America, Saddam no longer sits on the throne of Iraq and Osama-bin Laden no longer has a cohesive army of terrorists. Now it is time for the church to begin to see this opportunity to preach the gospel and go in and get the job done before the final prophetic scripture for the entirety of Iraq to be destroyed is fulfilled. WE MUST GO NOW!

What a tremendous challenge awaits us, but what a tremendous victory awaits the soul who find a living Savior, Jesus. Men's hearts are weary from war. Iraq's whole history is about brutal and ruthless wars. It has never stopped. Some of the early wars were so heinous that even after hundreds of years the animosity and hate for the invaders still resonates in the hearts of Arabs.

We have the true answer for them, God's peace. Let's not let this great opportunity pass us by. We have been given a mandate from God to go and preach this gospel to the whole world. Iraq is now open and willing, but how will they know unless someone such as an Abraham hears the voice of the Lord and tells them to leave this land (America) and go to a place He has filled with the promises of God. Jesus gave us instructions, He said, "GO." Knowing the signs that

Jesus promised would follow the obedient we are in for another book of Acts in Iraq!

> "Later he appeared to the eleven as they sat at the table; and He rebuked their unbelief and hardness of heart, because they did not believe those who had seen Him after He had risen.
>
> And He said to them, 'Go into all the world and preach the gospel to every creature.
>
> He who believes and is baptized will be saved, but he who does not believe will be condemned.
>
> And these sings will follow those who believe: In My name they will cast out demons; they will speak with new tongues;
>
> they will take up serpents; and if they drink anything deadly, it will by no means hurt them; they will lay hands on the sick, and they will recover.'
>
> So then after the Lord had spoken to them, He was received up into heaven, and sat down at the right hand of God.
>
> And they went out and preached everywhere, the Lord working with them and confirming the word through the accompanying signs. Amen." Mark 16:14-20 NKJV

Chapter Six

A Tale of Two Cities

Most Bible scholars understand Ezekiel 38 and 39 as the last days scenario of what takes place in Jerusalem and Israel with the nations that invade her. But, I believe as we read scriptures we shall see that our eyes should be on Babylon and Iraq just as sharply. Some fantastic scriptures state, in no minced down language, just what is going to happen in Iraq. We see the beginnings of Jeremiah 50 and 51 coming to pass. Jeremiah 50 and 51 is to Iraq what Ezekiel 38 and 39 is to Israel.

Why is it important to recognize how great a role Babylon and Iraq will play in the last days? When you search through scriptures you will find a tale of two cities, Babylon and Jerusalem.

JERUSALEM

- City of God
- Jesus was crucified there
- City of Promise
- Capitol of God's kingdom here on earth
- A city that must depend upon God
- God's eternal city
- City of peace

BABYLON

- City of man
- City of disobedient to the Word (Scatter)
- City of the beginning of the Times of the Gentiles
- City represents man's independence
- City of rebellion
- City of was
- City where wickedness resides (Zechariah 5)
- **City to be completely destroyed in the last days**

We find in these two locations some extreme differences, but all based on the scripture and what the Word of God says about each city and nation. When we look back at history we find that in 586 B.C. The Babylonians invaded Israel and in a ruthless and vicious battle Jerusalem was sacked and destroyed. Judah was no longer an independent nation and the Jewish people were taken into captivity.

Babylon was the nation that destroyed God's chosen people and God's chosen city. Not only did Babylon show no mercy, but also they destroyed Solomon's temple and removed the last line of Kind David to sit on the throne! Who ever made it through this onslaught was taken away and it is Psalm 137 that tells us how the people felt and what they prayed that day.

> "By the rivers of Babylon, there we sat down, yea, we wept when we remembered Zion. We hung our harps upon the willows in the midst of it. For there those who carried us away captive asked of us a song. And those who plundered us requested mirth. Saying, 'Sing us one of the songs of Zion!'"
>
> *Psalm 137:1-3 NKJV*

Here we see how ruthless the Babylonian invaders were and how they treated the captives without mercy. The Jewish people had just seen their land become a dust bowl, the temple taken to rubble and people murdered and viciously attacked before their eyes till nothing was left.

The enemy taunted them and demanded that they sing to their God about their beautiful city that was no more. When they say they hung their harps in the trees and wept, we see the total discouragement they were in.

As we go on in this Psalm we read:

> "How shall we sing the Lord's song in a foreign land? If I forget you, O Jerusalem, Let my right hand forget its skill! If I do not remember you, let my tongue cling to the roof of my mouth—if I do not remember you. If I do not exalt Jerusalem about my chief joy." Psalm 137:4-6 NKJV

The Jewish captives make a vow to themselves to never, ever get comfortable in Babylon and to remember and speak of Jerusalem always. One day when given the opportunity they will have the heart to go back because they have never forgotten. They believed God would not fail them.

Next they say:

> "Remember, O Lord, against the sons of Edom **the day of Jerusalem,** Who said, raze it, raze it, to its very foundation!"
> Psalm 135:7 NKJV

The concept of the day of Jerusalem is profound. What exactly is the *"day of Jerusalem"*? It's really a day that starts the clock ticking on this judgment to destroy Iraq. It is a time frame we can definitely look to and know that the hands on the clock are turning in prophetic movement. I believe the *"day of Jerusalem"* was a very specific time in 1967 when Jerusalem was back under the control of the Jewish people. Their prayer, *"next year in Jerusalem,"* echoing out over the generations, finally came to a reality. When Jerusalem came back into the hands of Israel the DAY OF JERUSALEM began.

They pray and cry out to God remember everything that the Babylonians did to them and to revenge them. It's hard to read what they say, but they were in extreme humiliation and pain.

They say:

> *"O daughter of Babylon. Who are to be destroyed, happy the one who repays you as you have served us! Happy the one who takes and dashes your little ones against the rock!"*
>
> Psalm 135:8-9 NKJV

They can't wait for the day when they will see the children of Babylon slaughtered as they saw theirs. War is a terrible thing and it takes the heart and wounds so greatly it is possible to think all manner of evil. Nevertheless, when you read Jeremiah 50 and 51 God makes it very clear, because of the terrible attack on Israel by Nebuchadnezzar, that he will revenge Jerusalem.

I believe the greatest gift God can give us is salvation. The Word of God is clear, He is not willing that anyone should perish. It is God's heart for man to receive the free gift of Jesus by confessing their sins and escaping the judgments. Iraq is finally today, in a position where the church can go in and a great revival can take place. That is why when God gives the warning that Babylon is to be destroyed—He says, *"And my people in the midst of her should get out."*

We are seeing a great thing right before our eyes with the reestablishing of Israel and Iraq, Jerusalem and Babylon. We need to take heed to the Word of God and we need to be observant and servants of the Lord in this very hour. There is a way to reach the heart of the Arab people with the gospel of Jesus Christ. God would not have allowed the destruction of Saddam and the liberation of Iraq unless He had a plan of salvation to the Arab people.

The question is what will your answer be? Will you begin to pray as never before for the underground pastors and believers? Will you commit finances to help churches willing to pay the price? Will you seek the Lord with your whole heart and let your families know we are coming to a close—and Jesus is about to return in full glory, honor, and power? Will you lead others to Christ because this is an hour of opportunity you might never have again? Will you realize the magnitude of pain and suffering that will take place when Babylon's judgment happens and be burdened with all your heart, soul and strength to get as many people into the Kingdom of God as possible? My prayer is that you will. I pray that this book will be a beginning of allowing people to realize where we are in the timetable of Bible prophecy and we will humble ourselves and pray. It will take the revelation of the holy Spirit to tell us when to get out of Iraq and we had better be obedient! Babylon will collapse quickly under the fulfillment of scripture by God's divine plan. Nothing and no one can change that. Read Jeremiah as he tells about that great and terrible day.

> *"At the noise of the taking of Babylon the earth trembles, and the cry is heard among the nations."* Jeremiah 50:46 NKJV

Babylon is going to collapse suddenly and in an instant. The scriptures tell us to wail over her and ask if she could possibly be healed, but the scripture is clear as to what will happen. Read with a sober mind and realize something the world has not even thought about is going to happen when it's least expected. Whether America will leave in time is up to us and if we come back to God as a nation!

The following selected verses from Jeremiah 51:1-64 are significant for our understanding:

> *"Thus say the Lord: 'Behold, I will rise up against Babylon, against those who dwell in Leg Kamai, a destroying wind.*
>
> *And I will send winnowers to Babylon, who shall winnow her and empty her land. For in the day of doom they shall be against her all around.*
>
> *Against her let the archer bend his bow, and lift himself up against her in his armor. Do not spare her young men;* **utterly destroy all her army.**
>
> *Thus the slain shall fall in the land of the Chaldeans, and those trust through in her streets.*

For Israel is not forsaken, nor Judah, by his God the Lord of hosts, though their land was filled with sin against the Holy One of Israel.'

Flee from the midst of Babylon, and every one save his life! Do not be cut off in her iniquity, *for this is the time of the Lord's vengeance; He shall recompense her.*

Babylon was a golden cup in the Lord's hand, that made all the earth drunk. The nations drank her wine; therefore the nations are deranged.

Babylon has suddenly fallen and been destroyed. *Wail for her! Take balm for her pain; perhaps she may be healed.*

We would have healed Babylon, but she is not healed. Forsake her, and let us go every to his own country; For her judgment reaches to heaven and is lifted up to the skies.

The Lord has revealed our righteousness. Come let us declare in Zion the work of the Lord our God.

Make the arrows bright! Gather the shields! **The Lord has raised up the spirit of the Medes. For His plan is against Babylon to destroy it.** *Because it is the vengeance of the Lord, The vengeance for His temple." Jeremiah 51:1-11 NKJV*

"Prepare against her the nations, with the kings of the Medes, its governors and all its rulers, all the land of his dominion.

And the land will tremble and sorrow; for every purpose of the Lord shall be performed against Babylon, to make **the land of Babylon a desolation without inhabitant."**

Jeremiah 51:28-29 NKJV

"Babylon shall become a heap, a dwelling place for jackals, an astonishment and a hissing, without an inhabitant.

They shall roar together like lions, they shall growl like lion's whelps." Jeremiah 51:37-38 NKJV

"I will bring them down like lambs to the slaughter..."

Jeremiah 51:40a NKJV

A Tale of Two Cities

"How Babylon has become desolate among the nations!"
Jeremiah 51:41b NKJV

"Her cities are a desolation, a dry land and a wilderness, a land where no one dwells, through which no son of man passes."
Jeremiah 51:43 NKJV

"My people, go out of the midst of her! And let everyone deliver himself from the fierce anger of the Lord."
Jeremiah 51:45 NKJV

"So Jeremiah wrote in a book all the evil that would come upon Babylon, all these words that are written against Babylon. And Jeremiah said to Seraiah, 'When you arrive in Babylon and see it, and read all these words,'" Jeremiah 51:60-61 NKJV

"Then you shall way, 'Thus Babylon shall sink and not rise from the catastrophe that I will bring upon her. And they shall be weary...'" Jeremiah 51:64 NKJV

Isaiah 13:19 says:

"And Babylon, the glory of kingdoms, the beauty of the Chaldeans' pride, will be as when God overthrew Sodom and Gomorrah." NKJV

Babylon play such an important part in the last days just before the return of Christ. We thought it was over for Babylon, but with a huge percentage of the world's oil supply and the coming on the scene of Saddam Hussein, Babylon was reborn and set on a course-like Jerusalem, of great prophetic fulfillment. The world is about to witness the truth of the Word of God. It will be like nothing we have ever seen and the warning is to get out with the new believers. MY PEOPLE, God says in the midst of her. God knows those that are His and He is just waiting for the church to harvest the field of Iraq. He loves the people of Iraq and wants to see them saved and delivered into His kingdom. How can they hear unless we understand why we are in Iraq and hear the voice of the Lord to TELL THEM.

Although we don't always understand the ways and means of God one thing is very clear in scripture, Jesus died to deliver us from sin, and the forgiveness that He offers is a way of escape in the world we find ourselves living in now.

> *"But know this, that if the master of the house had known what hour the thief would come, he would have watched and not allowed his house to be broken into.*
>
> *Therefore you also be ready, for the Son of Man is coming at an hour you do not expect.*
>
> *Who then is a faithful and wise servant, whom his master made ruler over his household, to them food in due season?*
>
> *Blessed is that servant whom his master, when he comes, will find so doing."* Matthew 24:43-46 NKJV

CHAPTER SEVEN

LOOKING BACK TO SEE THE FUTURE

Most Americans are not familiar with the history of Iraq. So to understand what is going to happen in the future with the nation, we must take a quick overview of the historical time line of Iraq. This is not meant to be a detailed history of Iraq, but a very simplistic review to orient the reader to some of the historical background information on Iraq that they might not be aware of.

In the beginning around 6,500 B.C., Iraq was basically agricultural. Around 4,000 B.C., the Sumerican civilization grew, invented, developed and became a strong intelligent people. They introduced writing in the cuneiform script. They were excellent mathematicians and brought in the rule of law. From around 1900 B.C. The empire is strong and rules for about 300 years.

An absolutely important date to remember is 586 B.C. Babylon invades Israel then and takes it to the ground, destroys Solomon's temple, removes David's seed from the throne and slaughters the inhabitants. Who ever remained alive was taken as a captive people to serve the Babylonians. Here is where Psalm 137 comes into play. The prayer that the Hebrew children cried out to God for was, in the day of Jerusalem, let Edom be remembered and avenge us.

In A.D. 637 Islamic Arabs defeat the Persians. Jump ahead to 1095-1192 and there were three major Crusades. Christian knights from Europe went out to conquer the Middle East, as it is known to the modern world today. These Christian Crusaders attacked Arabs in the holy cities, and really, left Baghdad of the equation.

From 1219-1227 Genghis Khan led the Mongols through central Asia and into what is now Iran, Iraq and Afghanistan. Genghis Khan and succeeding invaders were beyond the definition of ruthless. In one battle alone over 120,000 Arabs were speared, beheaded, and slaughtered. The average American couldn't begin to comprehend the vicious slaughter that took place!

When we learned of the beheading of the journalist Daniel Pearl, we were shocked and in disbelief. Now as more civilians have been beheaded we are horrified that we can watch the video on most Internet websites. As horrifying as the beheadings are to most Americans, the concept of video taping these heinous acts create a detestable and guttural reaction, likening these terrorists to less than an animal standard, in the minds of most Americans.

Under Genghis Khan and future invaders, all the irrigation systems that the Sumerians had developed to keep the Fertile Crescent full and producing were destroyed and the beautiful fields between the Tigris and Euphrates revert to a barren and bleak desert again. Essentially, the area dissolves into a wasteland, with different religious factions fighting one another and destroying what future they might have held as an unified nation.

Again, the fulfillment of the scripture with a prophetic plan said to scatter. Division breaks the purpose for prophetic purposes. Without unity there is no power. Power derives from a cohesive force. Unity provides the power to make sure nothing is impossible for you to accomplish, as God stated in Genesis over the Tower of Babel.

In 1258 the Mongols attack and loot Baghdad. And although great damage is done none of the catastrophic prophecies concerning Babylon even come close to this overthrow, showing us they are yet to come. In 1300 Timur returned to conquer Mesopotamia and the whole region falls into decay and desolation.

In 1281-1453, the Ottoman Turks rise to power and conquer Constantinople, which is the last Christian stronghold in the area.

Looking Back to See the Future

From 1501-1508, factions among the different Islamic beliefs start fighting and today the different Shia, Sunni, and Wahhab are what we see challenging the new government of Iraq. Najaf and Karbala are the same holy cities today, with constant fighting, as they were in the past. Again they are daily in the news. In America's war on terrorism, not a war with Iraq, and not as an invader, but a liberator—we still find the struggle to be over fundamental religious differences! Nothing has changed.

Finally, in 1516-1566 a Sunni, Suleyman the Magnificent, gains the control needed to rule Mesopotamia. During the years 1774-1792 the Ottomans are trying to retain power, but Sunnis are in Baghdad and Wahhabis are on the warpath to convert Shia's.

Around 1831, Bubonic plague hit Iraq and devastates the people. This plague was gruesome and had to run its course since no medicines or knowledge of how to stop it were available to the people. It was a horrible death and one the world should look back on and realize biological warfare should never be the weapon of choice!

Next, natural disasters hit the region. The Tigris floods and many of the mud buildings and the city buildings are washed away and destroyed. It is during this season that Baghdad becomes a real center of government. From 1831 through 1870, we see the influence of the Ottoman Empire declining and over ten governors reside over Baghdad. It is no wonder the control of Baghdad has been an important role for any one that wants to rule Iraq.

When American forces went into Iraq we knew without a doubt we had to take Baghdad and set up our influence and rule to make the liberation of Iraq a success.

As we come into the years of 1869-1918, we see Great Britain taking a major interest in Iraq. The Suez Canal is opened and the British take on a major role protecting the area to maintain control of the major sea routes to India. As World War I begins, it becomes apparent to Great Britain that they must control Baghdad. General Stanley Maude, told the Arabs that he had come to liberate them! Sound familiar?

The battle that the British had was not an easy win and there was a great loss of life. Thousands of British soldiers were held in Iraqi prisons. At this point in history the political position of the United States was not in support of Great Britain liberating Iraq! Great Britain, on the other hand, was smart enough to know that India, their precious treasure, and the oil, discovered in Iraq, was nothing to be left undone. It needed to be in the hands of a civilized nation and liberated for future use!

The Iraqi people helped Great Britain overthrow the Turks, but in no way did they want another foreign power to rule them after liberation was complete! The British came up with the idea of Air Patrol and used planes and bombs to stop the revolt and control the area.

In 1927 a major find which, would change the history and the economy of Iraq, of oil, the Kirkuk oilfield was discovered. This has turned out to be one of the largest oil finds in the world. Some have estimated that it holds 50% of the world's oil supply! Now, there was all the more reason for the Iraqi people to hate this liberating, but in their eyes, occupying power. Revolts turned into a national struggle for independence from Great Britain.

Eventually, Iraq was admitted to the league of Nations and on Oct. 3, 1932 Iraq become a nation independent of Great Britain and we begin to see again the Islamic factions within the nation trying to overthrow one another for power. In 1936 General Bakr Sidqi overthrows the government in Iraq in the first military coup. In 1958 the monarchy is overthrown and the royal family is slaughtered. In 1968 Baathists, along with Saddam Hussein overthrow the regime and 11 years later Saddam will become President of Iraq. In 1977 there were mass deportations of the Shiite Muslims to Iran because of the riots in the holy cities of Karbala and Najaf. The fundamental struggle is a religious one and has been for thousands of years.

On September 4, 1980, war begins with Iran and Iraq and both nations will fight each other for over eight years and lose over 1,000,000 men. Saddam has proven that be is not going to lose control of Baghdad, Iraq or be forced out of power. Even when he under-

Looking Back to See the Future 57

stands the tremendous loss of men and that almost every family has experienced such horror he claims victory! His regime is completely run by torture and brute force. Rape, murder and heinous tortures keep the people and the government completely paralyzed. No on threatened Saddam's power.

Saddam begins to develop nuclear weapons and on June 7, 1981, the world woke up to the shock that Israeli warplanes had attacked the nuclear reactor near Baghdad. Israel did the world a great favor by taking out Saddam's nuclear capabilities. As we can see in this present liberation of Iraq that was a fortuitous act.

In 1984 it became very clear to the world that Saddam was pure evil and that his use of chemical weapons against the Iranians was a drastic, terrible and reprehensible act. The world took not of the kind of leader Saddam was and began a process of sanctions against Iraq. They did little to stop Saddam from ruling or destroying the oil fields in the future.

August 2, 1990, Iraq invades Kuwait and the world is basically thrown into World War III. It took America about six months to prepare for war and they launched air strikes and an operation to liberate Kuwait under George Bush, Sr. Miraculously, this was done in about a 40 day time frame! Our military mission at that time was to liberate Kuwait, not Iraq. We left Saddam in power believing after such a great defeat that the people world finally take care of Saddam Hussein! What the world didn't know was the depth of fear the people had of him and how completely Saddam was still in control. So, he remained in power.

From 1990 to the present Iraq has defied the United Nations sanctions, U.N. Weapons inspections, and rejected every effort to operate in a decent and peaceful manner. We are now at war with terrorism in Iraq. Looking back at the history of their nation we are now seeing the same fundamentalist religious issues among the people of Iraq. This fighting is primarily between the Shia's Sunni's and Wahhabe's. The main goal will be to hold Baghdad, as the center for the new government. We must hold Najaf and Karbala because they are the cities with religious extremes, willing to do anything to overthrow the new government. With this religious revolt mentality only a strong central government will probably be able to control the extremism that is well documented with each group over the centuries.

The cities, such a Kukirk, known for oil and the ports that are needed to transport that treasure are well secured, or shall we say liberated, from the extreme factions. That's not to say that they won't have military struggles in the future. But for now it looks like a new Iraq will be built. A new central government will try to rule the nation in peace, but ultimately the problem comes back to a spiritual battle that will only be fulfilled as the prophecies of Jeremiah 50 and 51 and Isaiah 13 and 14 are fulfilled.

We do know what is going to happen, we just don't know when! We must understand these prophecies in order to recognize the time of departure from our liberation of Iraq. If we try to hold on too tightly America will pay a heavy price! While this is a very brief and basic historical background of the area we know as Iraq, I believe it was necessary to show how the region started, what is has gone through, and help to explain the wars and infighting that are just a part of the nation's history. What this means to America today I believe, will be seen in the future fulfillment of prophetic scriptures that show clearly a message of the future destruction of Iraq. These prophetic scriptures are an early warning to GET OUT, when we truly begin to understand the prophetic significance of Jeremiah 50 and 51 and what will happen to America if she remains in Iraq.

> *"And then Jesus went out and departed from the temple, and His disciples came up to show Him the buildings of the temple.*
>
> *And Jesus said to the, 'Do you not see all these things? Assuredly, I say to you, not one stone shall be left her upon another, that shall not be thrown down.'*

Now as He said on the Mount of Olives, the disciples came to Him privately, saying, 'Tell us, when will these things be? **And what will be the sign of Your coming, and of the end of the age?'** *And Jesus answered and said to them:* **'Take heed that no one deceives you.** *For many will come in My name saying, 'I am the Christ,' and will deceive Many.*

And you will hear of wars and rumors of wars. *See that you are not troubled; for all these things must come to pass, but the end is not yet.*

For nation will rise against nation, and kingdom against kingdom And there will be famines, pestilences, and earthquakes in various places.

All these are the beginning of sorrows.'" Matthew 24:1-8 NKJV

CHAPTER EIGHT

WHAT IS ABOUT TO HAPPEN IN IRAQ?

Isaiah 13 and 14 lay out a scenario for Iraq that is pretty frightening. Let's go through the verses and see what the outcome for the future really is. Isaiah is given a vision and he describes it as a great burden! He sees *"the day of the Lord"* and it is frightening and very disturbing to him. As you read Isaiah 13:1-9 you get a very scary picture of what is about to happen in Babylon and Iraq. In verse nine we get a summary:

> *"Behold, the day of the Lord comes, cruel, with both wrath and fierce anger, to lay the land desolate; and He will destroy its sinners from it."* NKJV

Let's take a look a what *the day of the Lord* actually is. As we read in scripture we know that this is a time of the last days and the fulfillment of final prophecy. We learn that in the latter days the antichrist will seek to destroy all of Israel and will be defeated and destroyed by Christ and His heavenly armies at His Second Coming. It will be a time when all prophecy that has been written, but as yet unfulfilled, will be completed and proven accurate. The Word of the Lord will come to pass just as it has been spoken and recorded.

Scripture is very clear about this day of the lord. It is a great day of the wrath of the Lord. The amazing plan of God is the grace that has been given to every person to receive Jesus Christ and escape this great and terrible day.

John 12:48 says:

> "He who rejects Me, and does not receive My words, has that which judges him—the word that I have spoken will judge him in the last day." NKJV

Romans 2:5 says:

> "But in accordance with your hardness and your impenitent heart you are treasuring up for yourself wrath in the day of wrath and revelation of the righteous judgment of God." NKJV

2 Timothy 1:12 States:

> "For this reason I also suffer these things; nevertheless I am not ashamed, for I know whom I have believed and am persuaded that He is able to keep what I have committed to Him until that Day." NKJV

The wonderful grace of God to keep us and protect us is given freely to every one who will confess their sins and acknowledge that Jesus Christ is the Son of God. It is really simple, but many will still not come to Jesus Christ because of the hardness of heart and because the lifestyle of sin has put them into bondage and the desire to sin is greater than the desire to know Christ. They are already under the deception that Jesus warned was coming and to make sure you didn't become a part of.

Revelation 6:17 says:

> "For the great day of His wrath has come, and who is able to stand?" NKJV

What is About to Happen in Iraq? 63

I can say, and I hope you can too, "I know whom I have believed and that He is able to keep me!" We are living in the perilous times that the Bible talked about and we need to turn immediately back to the simple truth of the gospel that America was founded on.

The Mayflower Compact is considered one of the first legal documents of America. The average history textbook in America tells you about the Mayflower Compact in generic terms, but won't let you actually read it because, as short as it is, it is rarely printed. What one learns when they actually read the document is that the purpose for coming to America and establishing a new nation was for:

(1) The glory of God
(2) The advancement of the CHRISTIAN FAITH
(3) For honor to their King

It is clear America was founded on the gospel of Jesus Christ and our history of this and other original documents make this uniquely clear.

America has had 234 years of grace from God. We have done many things wrong, but our original covenant is still standing. It was not until a few years ago, in Massachusetts, that we passed a law that was a breaking of our original covenant with God. The covenant to advance the Christian faith was nullified when we passed a law to allow homosexual marriage. This is a tremendous violation of the Word of God. Now, if America continues on this path she will be in a prophetic fulfillment of scripture that will bring America, as well as every other nation, to a day of the Lord. Which side of blessing or judgment we end up on is entirely dependent on wether or not we come back to the commandments of God.

There is a way of escape from the judgments and a way to heal our families and our nation, and that way is to repent and come back to the ways of the Lord. We can't say we look for the nation to do this. It is an one on one personal choice. The nation is you and I as individuals who must come to this place of repentance and then in great numbers we can again receive the tremendous blessings of our God.

This great and terrible day is also a great and wonderful new beginning to all those who find their lives in Jesus Christ by accepting the grace, forgiveness and protection He offers by accepting and believing in Him and Him alone.

Isaiah 13:11 states:

> *"I will punish the world for its evil, and the wicked for their iniquity; I will halt the arrogance of the proud, and will lay low the haughtiness of the terrible."* NKJV

This day of the Lord is a time that will be coming and I urge every reader to take the way of escape that Jesus Christ offers every living human being. There is absolutely nothing in your past that cannot be forgiven. If you have had the opportunity to see Mel Gibson's movie, *"The Passion,"* you realize what Jesus went through to save you and forgive you. This sacrifice of Jesus was for all mankind, to bring man back to the place of a right relationship with God and to give every man, woman and child the only hope the world has. It is my prayer that you accept this free gift of God through the reading of this book and turn to Him with all your heart, soul, mind, and strength.

As we continue with Isaiah 13 we see that Isaiah had a vision concerning Babylon. **This great and terrible time has Babylon at the center of it!** Verse six tells us to howl because Babylon and Iraq will be destroyed. Verse 19 tells us:

> *"And Babylon, the glory of kingdoms, the beauty of the Chaldeans pride, will be as when God overthrew Sodom and Gomorrah."* NKJV

Since, that has never happened in the history of Iraq we know that this is a prophecy about to be fulfilled as we see the signs warning us to look up for the coming of the Lord is at hand.

Verse 20 says:

> "*It will never be inhabited, nor will it be settled from generation to generation; nor will the Arabian pitch tents there, nor will the shepherds make their sheepfold there.*" NKJV

God's word is very explicit. Babylon and Iraq are about to come to the time of their destruction.

Verses 21 and 22 round out this prophecy:

> "*But wild beasts of the desert will lie there, and their houses will be full of owls; ostriches will dwell there, and wild goats will caper (dance) there. The hyenas will howl in their citadels. The hyenas will howl in their citadels, and jackals in their pleasant palaces.* **Her time is near to come, and her days will not be prolonged.**" NKJV

Isaiah 13 does give a clear warning that God says should be headed and that is found in verse 14:

> "*...Every man will turn to his own people,* **and everyone will flee to his own land.**" NKJV

The world has a coalition right now and many nations find themselves, along with America, in the land of Iraq. America should not assume she would escape this judgment if she decides to stay in Iraq. The warning is very clear every nation in Iraq is told to take the opportunity of grace and go home!

Isaiah 13 and 14, along with Jeremiah 50 and 51, lay out clearly for the reader what is going to take place in Iraq. God even gives us the information we need to realize who will be responsible for this destruction. Isaiah 13:17-18 says:

> "Behold, I will stir up the Medes against them, who will not regard silver; and as for gold, they will not delight in it.
> Also their bows will dash the young men to pieces, and they will have no pity on the fruit of the womb; their eye will not spare children." NKJV

This seems pretty cruel to the average American, but after watching the beheadings of several people in Iraq we now realize how ruthless and terrible humans can be when filled with pure evil that is unrestrained. This prophecy also fits well with what is taking place in Iran and surrounding Arab nations right now with the development of nuclear weapons. It is estimated that Iran is less than three years away from becoming a nation with nuclear weapons that could change the dynamics of the area!

Isaiah 14 brings in Israel and tells us clearly that God has chosen Israel and will have mercy on this nation. Verse one and two states it clearly:

> "For the Lord will have mercy on Jacob, and will still choose Israel, and settle them in their own land...
> ...and (they shall)rule over their oppressors." (only when Christ is returned will they have this kind of power). NKJV

Verses three through seven tell us:

> "It shall come to pass in the day the Lord gives you rest from your sorrow, and from your fear and the hard bondage in which you were made to serve,
> That you will take up this proverb against the king of Babylon, and say:
> 'How the oppressor has ceased, the golden city ceased!
> The Lord has broken the staff of the wicked. The scepter of the rulers;

He who struck the people in wrath with a continual stroke, He who ruled the nations in anger, is persecuted and no one hinders.
The whole earth is a rest and quiet; they break forth into singing.'" (Jesus will be ruling and reigning!) NKJV

There is coming a day very soon, when these two cities, Jerusalem and Babylon, are going into the last showdown. Jerusalem, the City of God, Babylon, the city of man are about to show the world which one is greater, mightier and which one will be the last one standing!

These two cities, Jerusalem and Babylon, are set as examples for us today to realize there is God's way, God's standards and God's expectations. Humanism is about to have its day, the day of the Lord!

There will be no effort, war or peace treaty that will stop the total destruction of Babylon and Iraq. Isaiah 14:24 says it distinctly:

"The Lord of hosts has sworn, saying, 'surely, as I have thought, so it shall come to pass, and as I have purposed. So it shall stand:" NKJV

Verses 26 and 27 bring home the point:

"This is the purpose that is purposed against the whole earth, and this is the hand that is stretched out over all the nations.
For the Lord of hosts has purposed, and who will annul it? His hand is stretched out, and who will turn it back?" NKJV

The complete destruction of Iraq and Babylon will happen. The warning is clearly given. America and every nation that is in Iraq, when they understand this prophecy, is to flee, get out of and return to their own land!

The question is will America know the time of the Lord and get out of Iraq? Or, will she remain—not believing the Word of the Lord and face the consequences of the prophecy about to be fulfilled?

> *"For the day of the Lord is upon all the nations is near; as you have done, it shall be done to you; your reprisal shall return upon your own head."* Obadiah 1:15

> *"For then there will be great tribulation, such as has not been since the beginning of the world until this time, no, nor ever shall be.*
> *And unless those days were shortened, no flesh would be saved; but for the elect's sake those days will be shortened."*
> Matthew 24:21-22 NKJV

CHAPTER NINE

WILL AMERICA HEED JEREMIAH'S WARNING?

The last chapter was a hard one to handle, but the scriptures are clear and it will happen. Take a look at Jeremiah 50 and 51. Jeremiah 50 opens saying:

> *"The word that the Lord spoke against Babylon and against the land of the Chaldeans by Jeremiah the prophet."* NKJV

Jeremiah 50 is interesting because it compares Israel and Iraq so there is no question about what is going to happen in both of those nations.

Verses two and three describe what is going to happen in Babylon:

> *"Declare among the nations, proclaim, and set up a standard; proclaim—do not conceal it—say, 'Babylon is taken, Bel is shamed. Merodach is broken in pieces; her idols are humiliated, her images are broken in pieces.'*
> *For out of the north a nation comes up against her, which shall make her land desolate, and no one shall dwell therein. They shall move, they shall depart, both man and beast."* NKJV

These verses make it clear what is about to happen. There has never been any event in Iraq's history where man or beast cannot dwell. We know this is a last days event and the circumstances the world finds itself in today are setting up the dominoes that are about to fall around the world.

Next, in verses four and five we read the scripture that deals with the promises to Israel.

> *"' In those days and in that time.' Says the Lord, 'the children of Israel shall come, they and the children of Judah together; with continual weeping they shall come, and seek the Lord their God.*
>
> *They shall ask the way to Zion, with their faces toward it, saying, come and let us join ourselves to the Lord in a perpetual covenant that will not be forgotten.'"* Jeremiah 50:4-5 NKJV

God is keeping His covenant promise of returning the Jewish people back to Israel. In May of 1948, that major prophecy was fulfilled and Israel became an independent nation. For Iraq that day came in October of 1932. It's interesting to note, that a new Iraq will begin with the democracy America is setting up and a new nation, perhaps the last, will come into existence. The next set of verses are a stern warning to the reader. The warning begins in verse 8:

> **"Move from the midst of Babylon,** *go out of the land of the Chaldeans, and be like the rams before the flocks."* NKJV

In basic English, get out of Babylon, Iraq, and be the first to leave! God's word couldn't say it much clearer. The question is will we be praying as a nation and know the right time. When our promoted assignment, remember the chapter on Shadrach, Meshach, and Abednego is finished, will we leave to try to stay and hold onto the oil, or the new prosperity we try to introduce to the world through the new government of Iraq? Will we get into bed, if you will, with the future Antichrist? The scriptures are so explicit here we dare not miss the warning. America, establish the new government and nation, bring the gospel to the people and then get out of Iraq! Verse nine tells us why we should leave:

> "For behold, I will raise and cause to come up against Babylon, an assembly of great nations from the north country. And they shall array themselves against her; from there she shall be captured. Their arrows shall be like those of an expert warrior; none shall return in vain." NKJV

In other words, their missiles will not miss and will hit every target. What kind of missiles, biological, chemical, nuclear, perhaps all three is the question? Verse 13 spells it out pretty accurately:

> "Because of the wrath of the Lord she shall not be inhabited, but she shall be wholly desolate. Everyone who goes by Babylon shall be horrified and hiss at all her plagues." NKJV

Verse 23:

> "How the hammer of the whole earth has been cut apart and broken! How Babylon has become a desolation among the nations! I have laid a snare for you;" NKJV

Verse 25-27:

> "The Lord has opened His armory, and has brought out the weapons of His indignation; for this is the work of the Lord God of hosts in the land of the Chaldeans. Come against her from the farthest border; open her storehouses; cast her up as heaps of ruins, and destroy her utterly; Let nothing be left. Slay all her bulls, let them go down to the slaughter. Woe on them! For their day has come, the time of their punishment." NKJV

Today we see that Iran, a nation that has been continuously at war with Iraq, has finally come to the place in their history where they can be a nation used to fulfill this dreadful prophecy. A nation on Iraq's border and now telling the world they are developing nuclear weapons. They will not be stopped. Until now, it would have been impossible to think of Iran having this kind of power. Within the time frame of about three years Iran will be a nation with nuclear capabilities that the world will have to deal with. The question is will Iraq pay the consequences?

Again, we see why this is going to happen and what God says about keeping His promise to Israel. Verses 33 and 34:

"Thus says the Lord of hosts:

> *'The children of Israel were oppressed, along with the children of Judah; all who took them captive have held them fast; they have refused to let them go.*
> *Their redeemer is strong; the Lord of hosts is His name. He will thoroughly plead their case, that He may give rest to the land, and disquiet the inhabitants of Babylon.'"* NKJV

Obviously, this is not a politically correct book! I cannot change what the Word says. It is apparent God has chosen Israel to preserve and Iraq to destroy. Don't get shocked at that statement because you must know the heart of God is the GOD IS NOT WILLING THAT ANYONE PERISH! I believe America has been drawn into Iraq just like Russia will have a hook put into its jaw to enter Israel (Ezekiel 38 and 39). We have a mission from God to find our hearts again and bring the gospel to this nation before it is too late.

America, you are carrying two swords right now. One, the sword of steel to move as an army to liberate a people who have been tortured, murdered, and oppressed by pure evil. But the other sword we yield is the "Sword of the Spirit" and we should be an army for the gospel's sake in this nation. We have been entrusted with the lives of these people in more ways than one. It is time to make the new constitution of Iraq live up to its principles that state in Article 7, "...This Law respects the identity of the majority of the Iraqi people and guarantees the full religious rights of all individuals freedom of religious belief and practice." (The Interim Constitution of Iraq).

If there was ever a time to go into all the nations and preach the gospel it is now! We should not fool ourselves, the evangelization of Iraq will not be without great sacrifice. But I believe God has a few extreme terrorists, like Saul, who are willing to kill for the faith, ready for a "Paul" conversion. There will be many, like Paul, who will be changed in an instant. I believe the miracles, signs, and wonders of Acts will take place in Iraq, because the love of the Lord never fails!

America, you have been given the two-edged sword. We must fight for freedom and liberty in the natural realm to create a free nation, but you must also fight in the spiritual realm to create a free man. We need to enter the fight and join with brothers and sisters in the underground churches of Iraq and pray for them as we have never prayed before. Many will have Peter experiences and be freed from the prison of bondage by the continuing and faithful prayers of the saints. Our finest hour has come!

"In you, O Lord, I put my trust; let me never be ashamed; deliver me in Your righteousness.

Bow down Your ear to me, deliver me speedily; by my rock of refuge, a fortress of defense to save me.

For You are my rock and my fortress; therefore, for Your name's sake, lead me and guide me.

Pull me out of the net which they have secretly laid for me, for Your are my strength.

Into Your hand I commit my spirit; You have redeemed me, O Lord God of truth." Psalm 31:1-5 NKJV

CHAPTER TEN

LIKE SODOM AND GOMORRAH DESTRUCTION COMES

God overthrew Sodom and Gomorrah for several reasons and we should take a small departure here to discuss those reasons. We come to Genesis 18 and find the discussion Abraham has with the angels of the Lord and come to the conclusion God would not destroy the city for 50 righteous people if found there. Abraham goes on with the pleading what if there is only 40, 30, 20, and the answer is, *"I will not destroy it for twenty's sake."* So Abraham pushes his luck and asks the same question about destroying the righteous with the wicked if perhaps there is only 10. It comes down to there just being Lot and his family who were given the warning to flee and Lot's sons-in-law who refused to heed the warning. So, the angels told Lot to get his wife and daughters and they would be led out of Sodom and Gomorrah to safety.

As in Iraq, some will make the choice and some will perish, not believing the Word of the Lord and thinking in the (politically correct humanism of the day). Some even reading this now cannot even conceive that Babylon could be destroyed suddenly and without remedy. But the Word of God does not lie and it is going to happen!

In the book of Jude we see apparent reasons for god's judgment on Sodom and Gomorrah. Verses 7-19 explain:

"...as Sodom and Gomorrah, and the cities around them in a similar manner to these, having given themselves over to sexual immorality and gone after strange flesh, are set forth as an example, suffering the vengeance of eternal fire.

Likewise also these dreamers defile the flesh, reject authority, and speak evil of dignitaries.

Yet Michael the archangel, in contending with the devil, when he disputed about the body of Moses, dared not bring against him a reviling accusation, but said, 'The Lord rebuke you!'

But these speak evil of whatever they do not know; and whatever they know naturally, like brute beasts, in these things they corrupt themselves.

Woe to them! For they have gone in the way of Cain, have run greedily in the error of Balaam for profit; and perished in the rebellion of Korah.

These are spots in your love feasts, while they feast with you without fear, serving only themselves. They are clouds without water, carried about by the winds; late autumn trees without fruit, twice dead, pulled up by the roots;

raging waves of the sea, foaming up their own shame; wandering stars for whom is reserved the blackness of darkness forever.

Now Enoch, the seventh from Adam, prophesied about these men also, saying, 'Behold, the Lord comes with then thousands of His saints,

To execute judgment on all, to convict all who are ungodly among them of all their ungodly deeds which they have committed in an ungodly way, and of all the harsh things which ungodly sinners have spoken against Him.'

These are grumblers, complainers, walking according to their own lusts; and they mouth great swelling words, flattering people to gain advantage.

But you, beloved, remember the words which were spoken before by the apostles of our Lord Jesus Christ:
How they told you that there would be mockers in the last time who would walk according to their own ungodly lusts. These are sensual persons, who cause divisions, not having the Spirit." NKJV

When you see what the people of Sodom and Gomorrah were like we can make a list that reads thus:

(1) There was practice of sexual perversion.
(2) There was a despising of the government and the rule of law.
(3) There was a passion to insult the rulers of the land.
(4) There were acts committed by people that corrupted themselves. They could not blame someone else.
(5) There was a strong belief in religious error and false doctrine.
(6) There was a practice of religion for purely reasons of financial and personal gain.
(7) There was hypocrisy in all the leaders and people, saying one thing, expecting everyone to do right, but in private and secret not living godly.
(8) There was an open practice of committing ungodly deeds.
(9) There was blaspheme of the true and living God.
(10) There were murmumrers and complainers about religion, government, sexual orientation, and all aspects of life.
(11) There were people living in ungodly lusts.
(12) There were people bragging and boasting about the ungodly and perverse lifestyle they were living.

(13) There were people that mocked the truth and would not speak the truth. They believed the deception of the age and would not hold to sound doctrine.
(14) There were people who lived their entire life to satisfy the lust of the flesh.
(15) There were people who would not listen to prophetic warning and rebelled and turned away from the warning.

It is easy to point our finger at other nations and see their sins so profoundly, but I wonder if anyone realizes from this list just how backslidden America has become? This last election of 2009 should show us how much name calling, lies and absolute efforts to tear down the system have gone on, so we can get our own way.

The pornography on the Internet, movies, and television have gone way past the mark of dignity or decency. It is an absolute revulsion the lust and the perversion that comes into the average American home through a personal home computer. We have seen religious leaders exposed, and fall fro high towers to the bottom rung of the ladder. We have a generation of youth rebelling from the teaching of the gospel and MTV does an excellent job to teaching the next generation how to be exactly like the scriptures in Jude said the last days would be like.

It is time for America to not just wake up, but get up. The 9-11 tragedy was not just a wake up call it was a—quit turning on the snooze button and get your keister out of that bed call!

It's not enough to be awake. YOU HAVE TO GET OUT OF THE BED AND PUT ON THE ROBE OF RIGHTEOUSNESS AND THE GARMENT OF SALVATION!

We are in Iraq, a nation that God says will be destroyed in one hour and suddenly. We are in a nation where we have a choice to make. Repent and declare that the kingdom of God is here, or continue in the state of immorality we are in and pay a very dear price! We will not escape the judgments of God because we are America. We will escape the judgments of God because we have accepted the saving grace of Jesus Christ and no longer live as the world lives! We do live in perilous times, but Jude 20 through 25 tells us what our hope is:

> *"But you, beloved, building yourselves up on your most holy faith, praying in the Holy Spirit,*
> *Keep yourselves in the love of God, looking for the mercy of our Lord Jesus Christ unto eternal life.*
> *And on some have compassion, making a distinction;*
> *But others save with fear, pulling them our of the fire, hating even the garment defiled by the flesh.*
> *Now to Him who is able to keep you from stumbling, and to present you faultless before the presence of His glory with exceeding joy,*
> *To God our Savior, Who alone is wise, be glory and majesty, dominion and power, both now and forever. Amen."* NKJV

We need to humble ourselves as a nation, seek God for His grace and understand the times we live in and make decisions based on the Word and with a clean heart.

> *"Now all things are of God, who has reconciled us to Himself through Jesus Christ, and has given us the ministry of reconciliation,*
> *That is, that God was in Christ reconciling the world to Himself, not imputing their trespasses to them, and has committed to us the word of reconciliation.*
> *How the, we are ambassadors for Christ, as though God were pleading through us; we implore you on Christ's behalf, be reconciled to God.*
> *For He made Him who knew no sin to be sin for us, that we might become the righteousness of God in Him."*
> *II Corinthians 5:18-21 NKJV*

CHAPTER ELEVEN

MY PEOPLE IN THE MIDST OF HER

"My people, go out of the midst of her! And let everyone deliver himself from the fierce anger of the Lord. And lest your heart faint, and you fear for the rumor that will be heard in the land (a rumor will come one year, and after that, in another year a rumor will come, and violence in the land, ruler against ruler)." Jeremiah 51:45-46 NKJV

It is no a stretch of the imagination to realize the rumors and the infighting for authority that has been going on in Iraq. Even when the election was held there was a jockeying for position behind the scenes.

We know from scriptures that the Medes (many say is modern Iran) are being prepared to be the instrument along with other nations to fulfill this prophecy. Jeremiah 51:28-29:

"Prepare against her the nations, with the kings of the Medes, it's governors and all its rulers, all the land of his dominion. And the land will tremble and sorrow; for every purpose of the lord shall be performed against Babylon, to make the land of Babylon a desolation without inhabitant."

NKJV

Verse 40 and 41:

"I will bring them down like lambs to the slaughter, like rams with male goats. ...How Babylon has become desolate among the nations!" NKJV

Verses 53-58:

"'Though Babylon were to mount up to heaven, and though she were to fortify the height of her strength, yet from Me plunderers would come to her,' says the Lord.

The sound of a cry come from Babylon, and great destruction from the land of the Chaldeans,

Because the Lord is plundering Babylon and silencing her loud voice, though her waves roar like great waters, and the noise of their voice is uttered,

Because the plunderer comes against her, against Babylon, and her mighty men are taken. Every one of their bows is broken; for the Lord is the God of recompense, He will surely repay.

'And I will make drunk here princes and wise men, her governors, her deputies, and her mighty men. And they shall sleep a perpetual sleep and not awake,' says the King, whose name is the Lord of hosts.

Thus says the Lord of Hosts: 'The broad walls of Babylon shall be utterly broken, and her high gates shall be burned with fire; the people will labor in vain, and the nations, because of the fire; and they shall be weary.'" NKJV

It *is* going to happen. When, only God knows, but we see the signs of the nation of Iraq restored, Israel is Restored, Saddam rebuilt Babylon and likened himself to Nebuchadnezzar and the day of Jerusalem, that Psalm 137 talks about, was in 1967, when the city came back under the control of Israel! We see the return of the Jewish people back to their homeland and we see the desert blooming in

Israel and twice now we have seen the nations come together to deal with the nation of Iraq.

We are in the midst of Iraq as I write and time is short. I believe we have a short period of time in which we should see Iraq growing and developing into a strong influence in the Middle East. In Daniel's vision of the statue the head represented the Babylonian Empire and then down the body we see the Medes and Persians, the Greek, and the Roman Empire. The statue will be standing before the Stone comes to destroy it. Iraq is standing and a new government is about to start the last and final course of prophecy. What an exciting time to be living in.

It is a spine tingling time to be living in and we should realize we need to be looking up for our redemption draws nigh!

Jeremiah 51:60-64 seal the prophecy for us to understand:

"So Jeremiah wrote in a book all the evil that would come upon Babylon, all these words that are written against Babylon.

And Jeremiah said to Seraiah, 'When you arrive in Babylon and see it, and read these words,

then you shall say "O Lord, You have spoken against this place to cut it off, so that none shall remain in it, neither man nor beast, but it shall be desolate forever."

'Now it shall be, when you have finished reading this book, that you shall tie a stone to it and throw it out into the Euphrates.

Then you shall say, 'Thus Babylon shall sink and not rise from the catastrophe that I will bring upon her. And they shall be weary.' Thus far are the works of Jeremiah." NKJV

As you read this book I ask you to reflect upon your own life and make sure you are IN CHRIST.

When we look at Matthew 24 and see all the signs coming to pass:

- ❏ Wars and rumors of wars

- ❏ Nation rising against nation
- ❏ Kingdom against kingdom
- ❏ False Christs
- ❏ False doctrines
- ❏ Famines
- ❏ Pestilence
- ❏ Earthquakes
- ❏ Persecution
- ❏ Iniquity abounding
- ❏ Love of many waxing cold
- ❏ Waves and the seas roaring
- ❏ The Gospel Being Preached In All The World for A Witness To The Nations And Then The End Shall Come!

The end shall come when we preach the gospel to the entire world. We have a great opportunity for Iraq right now. With satellites and television, Internet, radio and good old-fashioned pastors, willing to go, we can reach Iraq and the Middle East quickly. Realize what is flying around in the heavens speaking to the whole world through fantastic technology—we can see and understand Psalm 19 a little better:

> *"The heavens declare the glory of God; and the firmament shows His handiwork."* Psalm 19:1 NKJV

The satellites in the heavens are declaring, speaking and showing the glory of the Lord daily.

> *"Day unto day utters speech, and night unto night reveals knowledge. There is no speech nor language where their voice is not heard."* Psalm 19:2-3 NKJV

It is absolutely amazing when you see pictures of tribes in the deserts of the Middle East and see satellite dishes. In the old cities the dishes cover the roofs and the Christian message is going into the Muslim nation at this very moment in the language of each family being reached. This is a 24/7 deal and:

> *"Their line has gone out through all the earth, and their words to the end of the world. In them He has set a tabernacle for the sun, which is like a bridegroom coming out of his chamber, and rejoices like a strong man to run its race."*
>
> Psalm 19:4-5 NKJV

This technology sends out the lines of communication to the whole world and for the first time in history the world can receive news and THE GOSPEL instantaneously.

There is coming a time very soon when the King of Kings and the lord of Lords will come through the heavens and take us home to be with Him forever!

> *Its rising is from one end of heaven, and its circuit to the other end; and there is nothing hidden from it heat.*
>
> *The law of the Lord is perfect, converting the soul; the testimony of the Lord is sure, making wise the simple;*
>
> *The statues of the Lord are right, rejoicing the heart; the commandment of the Lord is pure, enlightening the eyes;*
>
> *The fear of the Lord is clean enduring forever;* **the judgments of the Lord are true and righteous altogether.**
>
> *More to be desired are they than gold, yea, than much fine gold; sweeter also than honey and the honeycomb.*
>
> *Moreover by them Your servant is warned, and in keeping them there is great reward.*
>
> *Who can understand his errors? Cleanse me from secret faults.*

Keep back Your servant also from presumptuous sins; let them not have dominion over me. Then I shall be blameless, and I shall be innocent of great transgression.

Let the words of my mouth and the meditation of my heart be acceptable in your sight, O Lord, my strength and my Redeemer." Psalm 19:6-14 NKJV

Iraq and Israel are the two nations to watch. Babylon and Jerusalem are the two cities God has promised to deal with and bless. We must pay attention closely to the time frame we are in under grace in this nation. We must present the gospel at all costs to win a people God is not willing to perish, and we must flee out of the midst of Babylon when understanding comes or we perish in her midst!

Only if America comes to repentance and prayer will she know and understand the times she lives in. We must not miss this great opportunity to reach the nation of Iraq with the gospel, to prepare a new nation for its place in the last days and to know when to obey God and leave! We cannot be like Lot's wife and look back for anything in Iraq. We must go!

"We then, as workers together with Him also plead with you not to receive the grace of God in vain.

For He says:

'In an acceptable time I have heard you,
And in the day of salvation I have helped you.'

Behold, now is the accepted time; behold, now is the day of salvation." II Corinthians 6:1-2 NKJV

As an author, educator, and counselor for over thirty years, Susan K. Reidel has authored numerous publications and study materials about Christian living and personal growth, leadership development, prophetic issues relevant to the Body of Christ, and in-depth Bible studies for those preparing for ministry.

Susan K. Reidel maintains an active speaking schedule, providing dynamic presentations about Christ's active role in the life of every Christian and the relevance of current events to end-time prophetic issues.

For booking:

Susan K. Reidel
7822 E. 100th St.
Tulsa, OK 74133

E-mail: sreidel@hotmail.com

Clip ✂ and remove to mail

To order additional copies of:

The Babylonian Prophecy
A Warning America Must Heed!

Please complete the information below:
(PLEASE PRINT CLEARLY)

Name: _____

Address: _____

City: _____

State: _____

Zip Code: _____

Phone #: _____
(PLEASE INCLUDE AREA CODE)

Email: _____

_____ Copies @ $10.00 each _____

Shipping and Handling @ $ 4.00 each _____

Total: _____

Make checks payable to: LOGOS TO RHEMA PUBLISHING

Mail orders to:

LOGOS TO RHEMA PUBLISHING
7822 E. 100th St.
Tulsa, OK 74133

Want to order online or order with a credit card?
This and other materials are available online now.

Are you a budding author?
Do you have a book inside you
Waiting to get out?
Logos to Rhema Publishing
Is the Answer!

We handle projects from initial editorial and marketing consulting all the way through to placement with national distributors.

Our services include,
but are not limited to:

Complete project marketing consulting
We want your book to succeed!

Editorial services:
•Evaluation of your text
Get feedback from a pro!
•Copyediting •Ghostwriting •Proofreading

We also offer:
•Book Cover Design
•Book Interior Page Design and Layout
•Prepress •Print Brokering
•E-book development for online access

And:

We can make your book
a fully produced Audiobook!
Complete with professional narration and sound

Contact us online at: logostorhema.com
Or email Susan K. Reidel at: sreidel@hotmail.com

www.ingramcontent.com/pod-product-compliance
Lightning Source LLC
Chambersburg PA
CBHW060407050426
42449CB00009B/1931